One Woman's Cry Is
Another Woman's Answer

One Woman's Cry Is
Another Woman's Answer

From Pain to Purpose

ROSEMARY C. GREEN

ONE WOMAN'S CRY IS ANOTHER WOMAN'S ANSWER FROM PAIN TO PURPOSE

NLT
Holy Bible, New Living Translation, copyright © 1996, 2004, 2015 by Tyndale House Foundation. Used by permission of Tyndale House Publishers Inc., Carol Stream, Illinois 60188. All rights reserved.

NIV
THE HOLY BIBLE, NEW INTERNATIONAL VERSION®, NIV® Copyright © 1973, 1978, 1984, 2011 by Biblica, Inc.® Used by permission. All rights reserved worldwide.

AMP
Copyright © 2015 by The Lockman Foundation, La Habra, CA 90631. All rights reserved. For Permission To Quote information visit http://www.lockman.org/

KJV
KJV Bible Citation on copyright page:
Scripture taken from The Holy Bible, King James Version. Cambridge Edition: 1769; King James Bible Online, 2017. www.kingjamesbibleonline.org.

iUniverse books may be ordered through booksellers or by contacting:

iUniverse
1663 Liberty Drive
Bloomington, IN 47403
www.iuniverse.com
1-800-Authors (1-800-288-4677)

ISBN: 978-1-5320-2106-0 (sc)
ISBN: 978-1-5320-2107-7 (e)

Library of Congress Control Number: 2017905016

Print information available on the last page.

iUniverse rev. date: 05/18/2017

Contents

Introduction

For everything that was written in the past was written
to teach us, so that through the endurance taught in the
Scriptures and the encouragement they provide we might
have hope.

—Romans 15:4 NIV

May the God of hope fill you with all joy and peace as you
trust in him, so that you may overflow with hope by the
power of the Holy Spirit.

—Romans 15:13 NIV

The Bible will always remain the only authority for fighting the enemy; we can hear the true voice of the living God in His Word. The Holy Spirit will keep His promise, and God's Word will never returned void. It is written in blood!

His powerful Word created the heavens and the earth, including you and me, so we should use His Word to change our lives; it is ours to use. We are the beneficiaries, and the hope of glory is real.

The title of this book stems from my sharing my testimony of everyday life with others and seeing the results of hope. It became easier to be transparent every time I shared my testimony. I shed burdens I had been carrying around for years, and I was able to ask forgiveness of those I hurt and forgive those who hurt me; I healed wounds that had lain dormant in my heart by my love. I regained a sense of fellowship that I had lost. I chose to forgive me first, which was hard. But we must forgive ourselves, our families, friends, churches, communities, leaders—the list goes on.

Free your freedom! That's a saying I came up with when I discovered my freedom. Here are simple but powerful words that helped me start forgiving others. Healing begins with a pure heart. "Dear God, please forgive me for those I've hurt, misunderstood, and didn't give a chance to love me. I'm sorry, and I ask Your forgiveness." I own my part of the pain. I believe God forgives me and fills in the blanks in my relationships whether they continue or end.

The seriousness of your repentant mind and faith helps you trust God to pick up the pieces and put them in place. When I tried doing that myself, I found myself picking up the pieces again and again.

Pain has a way of separating facts, leaving foundations shallow, and clouding memories. You must own your part no matter how hard that is. You will end up in a position where healing begins and you receive God's blessings. His knowledge and wisdom bring clarity to our lives and healing to our pain.

Decree forgiveness for yourself, and give God praise and thanks! Walk away knowing He's a forgiving God and that you are forgiven. The prayers of the righteous avail much, amen and shalom.

As I shared my testimony, I saw it affect others. So many of us are in secret pain, but we all must continue the battle of life. The clock keeps ticking, life is moving forward, so we must consciously move with it. Our family, friends, jobs, and many other concerns put demands on our time and emotions. We have to prioritize what is important to us and avoid creating unhealthy attachments and conflicts.

Because of my pain and disappointment, I always felt I didn't fit in with life; I was vulnerable to responding to others' needs. My faith taught me what I could do and what I couldn't do, but I still had questions about how to do what was right. I wanted to do what was right, but at times, I was frustrated in spite of the smile I wore. There were many things I wanted to say and do but didn't. I simply pushed my pain way down until it became silent. Fear gripped me, as did a sense of rage and shame.

My journey began because I wanted out of the silent rage of frustration called pain. But I felt alone and was afraid I would be that way forever. I felt like the walking dead. I knew I wanted to be free, but I didn't know how to gain freedom within. I came to realize we can be out of prison but still bound with chains. Our chains can be a sense of madness, disappointment, and rage, and the biggest chain can be unresolved memories.

I had questions I asked myself about those I saw around me especially after I became a Christian: *Why are people telling me to do something they aren't doing? Did God say this? Are these God's rules or their rules? Why do they have to change me instead of God, whom I serve? Where is that in the Word? Is that really Bible, or is it jealousy?* I wondered what was real and what was not. I would think, *Come on, God! I want You because I need You! What is all this? How many times do I have to push this stuff down? What do I do with all this pain I came to You with?*

You get the picture. These questions never really stopped; they just changed as I matured into the things of God. If I can help you avoid a bad season in your life, grow, and mature, I want to. I have forgiven those who were supposed to be my mentors in this matter. Pain is real, but it can be challenged by truth. Truth takes the high road, and it will always shine light on every lie.

My personal testimonies, including being healed of cancer at age nineteen, have reached many people. As I shared my story on radio and television, I was amazed at how God used my story for His glory. As God was healing me, I was learning of others dealing with some of the same things, and that was shocking. The enemy repeatedly told me I was crazy for sharing my story. He tried to convince me people would learn my business and use it against me.

The amazing revelation is that the more I shared, the more I was being healed and people were being freed. I'm not the only one going through this type of pain. I can hear people crying through their smiles because of their deep-seated fears. It's okay. Jesus is the answer. Let Him connect you with the right person, and you will soon find out that someone else has cried for the same reason you are crying. Be comforted as you read the transparency of the stories I share in this book.

The detours and adventures we experience in life are our testimony. As we lay down our lives in love and become transparent and vulnerable, we are reminded of how Jesus lay down His life for us! What love the Father has for us that He sent His only Son to die for us. We have hope in Jesus.

If for some reason you are ready to share your story to help someone else to see God, please feel free to contact us because *One Woman's Cry Is Another Woman's Answer.*

Dedication

But seek first the Kingdom of God and His righteousness,
and all these things will be given to you.
—Matthew 6:33 KJV

But seek (aim at and strive after) first, of all His kingdom and
His righteousness (His way of doing and being right), and
then all these things taken together will be given you besides.
—Matthew 6:33 AMP

And He will give you all you need from day to day if you
live for Him and make the Kingdom of God your primary
concern.
—Matthew 6:33 NLT

But seek first His kingdom and his righteousness, and all
these things will be given to you as well.
—Matthew 6:33 NIV

Therefore do not worry about tomorrow, for tomorrow will
worry about itself. Each day has enough trouble of its own.
—Matthew 6:34 NIV

I thank the Lord for the opportunity to express myself with such freedom, hope, and faith. Because of that, I dedicate my life to serve Him in spirit and in truth, and I am enjoying the journey. Through it all, Jesus is with me, and He loves me. Jesus, I love you!

I thank my wonderful and one-of-a-kind man of God and loving spouse, Arthur Green Sr. His patience is priceless. The peace that surrounds him overflows into my life and has given me the opportunity to be a total woman. I can express my cries, joy, and love to him without fear. His security in the Lord upholds me and our family to be all that God has purposed us to be. His prayers and covering has brought such revelation to every step that I make in the Lord as a woman of God, spouse, and mother. We have been married for over thirty-nine years, and not only do I love him, I also like him, which is so biblical. This allows me to read God's Word with life's clarity due to the life he lives. Thank you, God, for Arthur, my chosen spouse!

I thank my children for their time, love, and patience. I thank them for allowing me to share God in our home and community. What love has the Father bestowed upon me through your love and support. Each one of you was planned and thought about before your birth! When the enemy tried to keep your births from happening, God overrode death and spoke life into my womb. Then the most beautiful thing happened to me—each of you was born so close to the dates planned. I thank God for trusting us as your parents. I love each of you and glad you are here. For that, I give Him all the glory!

I want my precious grandbabies to know that Memaw loves you! You will always be special in my heart. You all are Rosemary's grandbabies. Each of you was chosen by God!

I thank my loving family and friends for their love, support, and patience for me to finally get this book out. Your prayers and support have been real blessings. You all know who you are. It's like birthing babies—with God's help, I'm pushing!

Foreword

I consider myself a blessed man to have such a woman as my wife. When I met her in 1975, I knew that there was something about her and that God had a plan for me.

God loves me so much that He blessed me with an angel, a true prophet, a woman who really loves the Lord.

Rosemary brings everything to life; she has brought such life to me, and as her husband, I trust God in her. From the time we met, she has been amazing to me. I didn't realize God has given her so much insight that allowed her to give out of her heart to you in this book about who she is.

Please read her words and listen to the words of God coming from her. The power and the wisdom in her is expressed in many ways. She's a wonderful mother and spouse, and I thank God every day for her.

In this book, you will see her heart for hurting women. This is one way you can share the little angel God sent to me. We were meant for each other. There is so much I can say about this woman of God and the way she loves her family and gives to God's people.

—Arthur Green Sr.

My mother, Rosemary Green, is a mighty woman of God. I believe in her ministry and what God is doing though her. As her daughter, I have been blessed to be involved in The Green Rose Ministries. This ministry has grown through the years and now includes dance, community outreaches, teas, and much more.

I have seen God move in our lives in so many ways. My mother inspires me to be a better woman, mother, and daughter. I also appreciate the love she gives to me and shows for her family.

My mother is a strong woman. My knowledge of what she has gone through has taught me how to handle my own children in good times and bad. I am a perfect example of how my mother handled different situations. She also allows my siblings, her grandchildren, and me to be ourselves. We make mistakes, but her love for us is unconditional.

My mom is very gifted in her ability to see others' talents, and she works hard to help others realize their talents and bring them out. She encourages others in this respect to become experts in their purposes and passions.

Many different women have been touched or inspired by my mother. As you journey into this book, I ask you to open your heart and mind, embrace her words, and let the healing begin.

—MyNeakka Green

If you want everlasting life, not just life, and if you're ready to change your life, this book will do exactly just that. Because of her strong will and mind, Rosemary is a strong woman.

Being who she is allows herself to open up to God. Yes, because she is drenched in righteousness, God—Abba, the Father—encourages her to let Him do great things through her with her evangelistic gifts.

Through her writing, she brings not just a message but also inspirational tributes to the life that I get to live among the examples she sets for herself, our family, and the world.

Rosemary Green isn't just my mother; she's more of a teacher, a confidant, a counselor, and an established author.

Congratulations on receiving this wonderful, insightful key to new life. Thanks to my mother, I'm very proud to say that I was birthed by godly greatness.

—Arthur Green Jr. (Ajae)

The pleasure and blessing I have of being able to have the advice of Rosemary Green as a mother and spiritual advisor is overwhelming. She is filled with inspiration, determination, and strength that can be defined only by her connection with God. Her wisdom and knowledge of the spiritual realm and all things positive are just examples of the gifts my mother is willing to share with others.

This book will help you with your troubles in life and will help point out problems that you may have hidden or may not even know existed. Take the time to read this book, and let it sink in and feed your soul. Take time to listen and smell the Green Rose, a rarity that should be cherished.

—Armani Green

As a mother, I am filled with memories of our family having fun and laughing in spite of the hard times we went through. We would entertain each other so much. One time, when Rosemary was about four, we were at church. Rosemary was always willing to sing, and there she was up in the front of the church and singing, and her brother, David, was pulling on my arm trying to get my attention. "Mom! Look!" as he was pointing to her feet. I saw that she had her high-topped patent-leather boots on the wrong feet but was nonetheless tapping away as she was singing her heart out. David was laughing so hard, and to keep myself from laughing, I had to stand up and howl at her, "Sing it, baby!" "That's my momma!" she yelled back.

—Gloria Smith (my mother)

Author Mrs. Rosemary Green has been my personal mentor for over ten years. I have had the privilege of watching her closely in her daily life. I am a product of her Ministry of HELP!—Healing Everything Life Presents.

Mrs. Rosemary has been my mother figure, counselor, prophetess, teacher, trainer, and mentor. In her writings, she exemplifies the epitome of success in life. What you will read in this book will change your mind about the way life works. Satan, the adversary of believers, will try to blind you to the truth about God, yourself, and everything that pertains to the things of God, but Mrs. Rosemary reveals the lies of the enemy in this book. When you know the truth, the truth will set you free. This book will reveal truth that will bring you healing and deliverance. If you want your life to change, read this book. I guarantee you that you will never be the same again.

The desire of this prolific author is to see people live free. Prophetess Rosemary lives what she proclaims. She is fluent in the prophetic, and her prophecies are accurate. God uses her to reveal secret things and warn others out of love. Her genuine love and concern for people will be unveiled in this book, which will challenge you to dig deep in yourself and be honest about your struggles. You will deal with issues you may have been avoiding for years. Don't be afraid to face your innermost fears. I am a living testimony of this ministry.

—Celeste Amaris Clarke

Many times, we search for the answer to the "why" of life. Rosemary gives the answer in this book. It has been a pleasure and honor to be personally acquainted with Rosemary for over twenty-five years. Her friendship and womanhood in all areas of her life are exemplified in this book.

Rosemary is a spiritual compass who gives sound, effectual, fervent, and righteous counsel. As you turn the pages, you'll find revelation that is applicable to your life and the lives of others.

Words cannot express the deep gratitude I have for a friend with such a masterful skill at articulating the heartbeat of God. I recommend you read the book if you want your life back.

—Alana Garrett

Rosemary Green is a necessary prophetic voice for these end times. She helps the wounded, hurting, brokenhearted, unsaved, and sick souls find their destiny in Jesus Christ.

Her HELP! Ministry is a tireless voice to the nations. She is a writer of books, plays, and Bible studies, she teaches dance and theater, and she's founder of Many Green's Media Production ministry. I am excited to see what God takes her to next.

—Phyllis McGuyer, evangelist

Sister Rosemary Green is a dear friend and loyal comrade in the good fight of faith. She is a mighty woman of God who enjoys the rewards of obedience to our heavenly Father's Word. Her ministry allows so many to hear His voice, follow His lead, and have awesome adventures in His kingdom through her diverse and unique ministry to the Lord and His people.

Just watching the Lord work His majesty through her is a blessing, but we have done more than just watch! After all, taking dominion over the enemy's camp and restoring God's kidnapped children back to Him is not merely a spectator sport. Sister Rosemary rallies the troops and is not intimidated by others' gifts or talents but instead invites her fellow comrades to raise their swords and banners high, mount up, and ride out to meet the enemy on his own turf right alongside her as God's faithful servant. Iron sharpens iron for the battle.

Sister Rosemary's unique creativity in the performing arts, her writing, and her ministry of deliverance and prophesy demonstrate the hand of God in His colorful, multifaceted expressions of love, reclaimed liberty, discipleship, and restored destinies for His purposes.

Sister Rosemary is dead serious about taking care of His business and is riots of fun to do battle with; she is a faithful companion. I also acknowledge her remarkable husband, Arthur, and her children, who are all devoted to her and to one another. They have blessed me marvelously. They all join the battle with their own radical gifts and special talents.

As you read, view, or listen, enjoy the spirit of a warrior bride and the spirit of conquering. She exemplifies the kingdom of light and the joy of the Lord, our strength.

Agree with the Lord that all His lost and wandering children will return to Him in due season! May we hasten to the return of liberty and freedom in His perfect time. You go, sister girl! Keep on keepin' on in His name.

—Jean Shortsleeve (a comrade, friend, admirer, and former
    POW released from captivity in 1976 by His grace)

I met Rosemary Green in 1995. She is the most sincere, trustworthy, knowledgeable, and consistent Christian. She had been involved in the international Ministry Women Aglow for over twenty-five years. When she retired as vice president of outreach on the North Central Texas Area Aglow Board in 2005, she worked with women and young people. She has a degree in early childhood development, and she was very active as a certified court appointed special advocate (CASA) in Travis and Burnet Counties in Texas for a number of years. Rosemary and her husband, Arthur, founded CHOICE (Children Helping Others In Choosing Eternity) Ministries.

Rosemary is a highly sought-after minister and speaker nationally and internationally. She conducts retreats, outreaches, and other activities throughout the year. After all these years of ministry, she experienced a strong nudging by the Spirit to put her encounters and knowledge in print in *One Woman's Cry Is Another Woman's Answer.* Other books are soon to follow, and you won't want to miss any of them.

—Glenda Wilson

Chapter 1

When a Woman Really Cries
—Her Womb Speaks

When a woman really cries, something is definitely wrong. Her shedding tears is a serious matter. Her pain makes it hard for her to breathe. And it's a whole other matter if you are the one causing her to cry. This is when her womb speaks and draws attention to the fact that something is wrong. Her heart is ravished by her pain. At this point, it can be bad and quite painful. It's truly not a time to ask her questions or accuse her of anything.

Her groans are her attempts to protect the very thing she fears within. The anguish becomes reality she doubts she can control as her cries become deeper. You witness her tears falling down her cheeks uncontrollably and understand that pain drips out with her tears. Her head races with thoughts of revenge. She thinks, *I'll never let this happen again. Nobody will ever take me here ever.*

You wait for answers. You are frozen. Her groans turn into words and questions. You let out a yelp! You know enough to let her be and give her space and time. Due to the severity of her cry, you just listen. You make yourself available in a caring way. You are creatively silent. You know you should step away from the tears but remain close.

You don't touch her or talk to her. You don't understand anything at this point. So you stop, look, and listen. You realize she will direct you from here with her actions and words. You do not judge her. Her pain is real. It is evident in her tears. You care for her, but helping her at that time can be a task. Anything can happen. The situation can instantly change or even become physical. You restrain yourself and listen to her breathing. You start praying for her; you want her to find peace in the midst of war!

What has offended her deeply is playing out in her head, but you know this too shall pass. The thought pattern increases by varied beats and sounds of defeat ready to respond. *This too shall pass* are the words that try to drown out the overflowing of tears that don't seem to stop!

Hours can go by. Time can be manipulated. Your racing thoughts are challenged by what has brought you to that place of disappointment initially. That's why your pain has to be lessened by your love for God. You have to let go enough to accept the truth of the cry you are crying.

Many people have reached this place and caused harm to themselves or others. The newspapers and jails are filled with this type of unsolved mystery and pain. Believe this—murder and hate are not the answer. On the other side of that place, many have found hope and love through Jesus, family, and friends, and they climb the ladder to their purpose and now testify and share their horrific experiences.

Do away with the rest of the cry that evokes pride that holds you captive. Let it go after you've gotten the bitterness out of the cry because it can eat you alive while the other party has moved on and does not recognize your tears. Burn your grave clothes and release its stink. Rid yourself of the could haves and would haves along with the what-ifs. They can stunt your growth and keep you immature and trapped.

Wake up and receive freedom. When you cry so hard that you become sick and your womb feels raw, get up and fight back. Shed your tears; that will allow you to find happiness again. God will bottle your tears and send you a season of unspeakable joy that is full of His glory when He heals you. He cries when we cry and laughs when we laugh.

Jesus cared about you enough to lay His life down for you and rise from the dead. The Word of God will help you reach your life goals that were established even before you were in your mother's womb.

We are quick to say we are all grown up, but we cry about the same things we prayed for yesterday. Should we pray for something different or cry about something different to confuse the devil? The insanity of this robs you of your identity in Christ. The enemy loves when you feed into this behavior. Don't get me wrong, though—crying is a very serious matter and tells us something is wrong.

Which takes me to the happy cry. We need more of this type of cry because it is as good as medicine. The Bible says a merry heart does good like medicine does. Think about how the enemy tries to turn anything good into bad. Look at our world today—good is bad, and bad is good. Life can be as exciting or as ruthless and deadly as you perceive it.

You can choose how to handle the horrific cries of life that come your way. Don't allow your fears to take you constantly on detours when you can embrace the pain and change. God is much bigger than everything you deal with. Try giving Him all of you along with your deepest cry, and go ahead—fulfill your purpose for life and live.

The enemy doesn't want you to realize how much you can handle in life. Work hard at who you are and are called to do. People will talk, and things will happen, but with Christ on your side, you will recognize you are walking out what's already won. When you go back to the simplicity of God's Word and wrap life up in it, the pain is much less and the happiness is much greater.

God protects you in your innocence even when you are abused. The keeper of righteousness always has a plan and never will run out because someone selfishly invaded your privacy and broke you down. That is not who you are; your name isn't Pain or Crybaby. Your real identity is in Jesus, and He's protecting it for you until you are ready to step up and claim it back.

You will experience healing if you are robbed of your innocence by the evil one. God sees everything and knows all. Vengeance will be His. If you are the victim of abuse, God will wrap His hands double around you. He cares about what happened to you no matter how bad it was. You are His child, and it is wrong for anyone to abuse you emotionally, spiritually, physically, or mentally. Who are they that we call them Lord? If it bothers you and it changed you, get up close and personal with God. He doesn't want your view of your purpose clouded.

Crying is a reaction to pain, but God, the healer, is the answer to your pain and tears. The devil has told you lies to trap you and hold you hostage to the pain in self-righteousness. This is the reason you are the way you are; you can lose your identity to the demon, who laughs at you. The devil is a lie.

No one wants to be in pain and hurting 24-7. Keep it real. Crying gets attention; it can lead to joy or sadness. What you are crying about can affect the path you take. Even when you're crying silently, some of us can still hear and see you. That's what led me to ministering through HELP!—Healing Everything Life Presents.

I never wanted to be a minister; I just wanted tell people about Jesus and what He did for me. I kept hearing people calling for help, but I would see them smiling and laughing. I couldn't get away from the calls for help all around me; I couldn't drown them out. That would bother me for years until God challenged me.

In this book, you will hear more of that story and the cries of those people. Jesus died for it all, big or small—it doesn't matter; if it troubles you, it troubles Him. What love He had to lay down His life to remove all pain and scar tissues! His Word is true, and it works if you work.

It really bothers me as God's servant to see people hurting and unable to find their way out of their pain. They've drowned themselves in their painful stories and gathered cheerleaders who manipulate them and play into their emotions with a tagline of a financial burdens added to their troubles as they seek help. You are to give honor to whom honor is due; a workman is worthy of his hire. But to be manipulated and controlled to do and operate is witchcraft and the spirit of Jezebel. You have to be aware of the wolves in sheep's clothing on all levels dealing with pain and hurt.

At some point, you must stop sobbing and ask questions before the pitfall. You might be broken down, but you will later be built up and give God glory. Bitterness is cancer, and it can kill you if you live in it. I've been there through no fault of my own. I had to own my part of sinking into bitterness because of folks. I owned it, and I asked forgiveness and moved on. But *bam*, there it was again but on another level. Thank God I was able to take the high road. It wasn't easy at first, but the more I love on Jesus and draw closer to Him, the more I want to obey even if I don't understand it all. We always land on our feet standing for sure.

The experience of course is a priceless favor. Cry it out and pray for the Holy Spirit to help you and stay on the narrow road. It will cost you something, but it will truly help others, and that's what you want. That's a blessing. Don't you dare let your tears be wasted time. Walk it out! You are worth it, and maybe one day, we will hear your story.

Prayer helps a lot and increases your chances of helping others. Sharing is caring when done in the right spirit. One woman's cry is another woman's answer. Don't let your tears be in vain.

Crying is so much different from shedding a tear or tearing up! It tends to hold you hostage to the pain that's registered for whatever reason. The hang-up is when you stay in it and the pain of the "Oh me! Oh my!" syndrome. Feeling sorry for yourself and manipulating others to be drawn in are wrong. It can be a toxin brewing inside you when no one is listening to your story. Purpose-driven, born-again people are focused, not distracted.

Keeping the love flowing will distract the enemy. Do not fall into the blame game when you're in pain. Own your pain but then release it with the understanding that this is what you're doing. It's not fair to those who care for real and want to help you. God has good people with good hearts no matter what anyone says. He has a ram in the bush that will take your place.

I've ministered to many people, and this is what I've observed. When you need to comfort a woman when she cries, be focused totally on her if the atmosphere permits. Keep her in view and listen to her. Then with much prayer and a caring heart, secure her with much love not to baby her but to really care for her. When a woman is broken, her view of things tends to automatically narrow down to the pain. You might not know how long it took for her to get to the boiling point; you have to move slowly toward talking about it gracefully. Keep in mind already everything possible has been discussed in her mind—the good, the bad, the ugly, and the truth. In a roundabout way, you weren't listening and didn't hear her in the beginning or didn't get it when she was relating to you. She is saying something to you and is very tired of repeating herself or dealing with the same thing with no changes.

She's about to fix it. Her pain is the root of what is being expressed depending on the wait and how long it's been hurting. Usually, it takes a while to get to this point of agony where the hurt turns into a groaning, swollen eyes, and a messed-up face, all signs of the enemy's snares.

All your emotions are on speed dial, and your anger is going full blast. The disgusting feeling of facing hurt with the mixture of truth can change the temperature and create madness. Already, she hates to cry in this zone of disgust. You don't know for sure that she is still to be heard, whether it's a private or a public cry for help. The idea of being out of control is aggravated by thoughts that ramble in her head. Woman, you are set free! Your story gets told, somebody hears you, and you come out of their pain. How amazing is that?

Take your authority back and grab your life out of the hands of the enemy. Own your part of your pain and trust God to bring you through. Don't toil with what's fair when truth is your platform to build again. Like it or not, help is here to pull you out of the shadows of pain. Share your story and help that person who is still hiding in grief at a no-hope bar. Break through her tears with the tears you've cried. You fellowshipped with pain and raged in the dark cloud of sadness. Don't be afraid to stretch yourself into the shape of His heart. Love with liquid dripping down your face onto your fabrics of shame to reach the light of truth. Truth shines light on the pain and offers you the key to get out of there. Change your life and grab your identity. Allow God to restore everything the cankerworms and the locusts have eaten. He will grow your bones and strengthen your life for the good. So embrace change and accept your newness whatever that may be.

We women say we want to change, but do we really? Stop kicking and screaming at your destiny. God sees everything you are facing, even the little foxy. You are making it hard on yourself, and your hurts can drag you down. It's not fair to yourself to lug them around so the world can see and judge you. People see what they care to see, so we are to pray. Prayer releases toxins that poison your mind with ungodly thoughts of revenge.

The enemy would love to control your mind and leave you stranded. Wake up, sleeping beauty, and put on your armor because you are in battle! Your fight has already been fought for you by Jesus, and you are victorious in His name.

Preparing yourself for greatness is a joy. Release your hurt. Forgive others for they know not what they do. After you cry your last tears, be done with them and don't ever visit that situation on that level again in Jesus's name! Fight the good fight of faith and know what you are doing here. It's more than believing; it's a lifestyle of faith. It's one of the major tools in the battle. We must keep marching—pick them up and put them down—until He shows up and tells you what to do next. Cry and wipe your tears, and keep up the fight because some things you will see no more. Repeat it as many times as you like until you believe it and own it. Put your name next to Jesus. Your best friend is the Savior of the world!

God fashioned us as women to bend and be flexible, but which way is another subject. We can carry life in our shapely bodies that stretch and move until we hear the beauty of a voice crying out of us. It's a miracle. You have heard the saying "Too blessed to be stressed." The influence God has given us women is incredible; it's nothing to play with or manipulate. God will bring you out without a scent of smoke on you if you obey His command and live right.

To the women in battle right now, I say, "This is almost over. Believe that!" You are to be encouraged and know that God heard your cry. It's no surprise to Him that you're dealing with this situation. He got you! When those tears are rolling down your face, remember that He's bottling them up and will turn them into tears of joy because He loves you and hears your battle cry. Wipe your weeping eyes and do your dance. Throw yourself a party and call it your "Told You So" party, uh huh!

You can have the last laugh. You've probably been there facing this by yourself or without an understanding shoulder to cry on for a while. But God is faithful and true, and He knows every hair on your head; He has you! He has never forgotten you, my dear. His love stretched so wide until He stretched and died just for you and me. If you were the only one on earth, He would have still died for you. Now that's good news!

Don't listen to the enemy's lies. Let the Holy Spirit do His job; He will comfort and guide you into truth in His time. You will not be disappointed what you learn through your cries of pain especially when they allow you to help another woman. One woman's cry is another woman's answer.

You will win every battle if your mind has been transformed by God's Word. It is good yet humbling to surrender all, even that which you don't understand, to test the Word against itself as a believer. The Bible speaks about confessing and releasing, which are good for the body. Hope is alive! When a real woman really cries, she will come out stronger! She'll seek God's help! The real woman wants the real Savior! Shalom!

Chapter 2

My Story: Perfect Enough For Perfection —But Is It Right Enough for God?

I grew up in a small town in Louisiana. My mother was single at that time. I was born in a shack off the highway in the woods, a shotgun house (some of you might know what I mean). I would sometimes think of Jesus being born in a manger, and I could see Him winking at me as I smiled back in love identifying small beginnings on earth. My mother gave birth to me alone in this shack. Because we lived back up in the woods, it took a while for me to get to the hospital, and I almost died. I finally made it to the hospital just in time.

I was born with what they called a veil over my face; I was supposed to be able to see into the future—sometimes dead people and spirits. That is what I was told growing up. My grandmother was full of peace and God's love; she said it was a gift from God and it was to be used for God alone. Because of many spiritual interferences and challenges, I became very fearful, especially at night. I dreaded nights because of all the activities that went on that only I would witness. When morning came, it was as if nothing had happened. As I was just a child, that scared me. I couldn't figure it out. There was no evidence that I could tell others. The feeling of entrapment is the worst kind of silent fear.

My dreams seemed so real, and I would have visions when I was awake. Many times, what I saw in my visions later took place just as I had seen them. Yes, it was very scary, and I didn't understand it.

I would love to visit my grandmother Madea even though I didn't like being out in the woods. I could share my dreams and visions with her, and she would always comfort me and make me feel much better; she would make my fears vanish. But I kept on having dreams and visions.

I would tell her about the monsters, the ghosts, and the dead people I would see, and she never made me feel crazy or weird. She would always reference everything to God having made me in this special way for His use to help people. I would say to her, "But I'm only a little girl! Why would God choose me? How would He use me in such scary ways?" She would tell me that God must have trusted me to help His people even though the messages weren't always nice.

I trusted her words. I knew Madea loved God, and I loved her for that. God used her a lot in my life. I did embrace God's gift as a child starting with trusting that He gave my gift to me. I could feel the weight of this gift falling on me like a blanket of concern I had to do the right thing with. I didn't know what to do other than obey God. I knew that whatever my gift was, I had to use it for His glory.

Many in my family don't know about that part of my life because I kept it a secret; I was afraid I would see something bad concerning them and be blamed for the outcome. I knew God trusted me, and I did well thinking it was our secret unless something happened and I had to help; it would be very low-key until God took over more in my adult life.

I felt exposed in a weird way; I felt different. As a child, I was learning daily about the unexpected sort of speech. Hello to my sweet beginnings, right? I always felt a little different and out of place with just about everything around me. I felt I didn't fit in a lot of times, but I was sure I could get in and make myself fit in and be just fine. With this gift and my true love for people, I could always make it work, but it took some adjustments on my part.

Most of my life, I constantly adjusted until I completely shifted into a reality that I wasn't quite ready for. Something happened in that shift. I felt I was making everyone but myself happy. I became difficult to understand because of what I was seeing compared to what people were telling me. Learning to separate the difference in the school of hard knocks wasn't always without constant, silent tears. Being misunderstood seemed to be part of my DNA. Hidden anger and private pain stemmed from these issues and left designer scars.

Sometimes, my hidden anger would get the best of me. It would come oozing out at the wrong times, and I would want to be alone. Growing up, I felt I was being singled out to handle household chores no one wanted to do. I took on the responsibility of trying to keep the peace at almost any cost. I became the rescuer and a lot more.

On a positive note, that caused me to develop many skills that became helpful down the road. I am now multitalented and creative and enjoy working with people. But at that time of my life, I faced pain and rejection. Being in the South, I was picked on because of the color of my skin. People can be cruel when your pigment isn't what they would prefer it was. How sad is that for a young child to encounter and live out? Being left behind by outsiders not of my blood type was real for me.

We were taught in our house to love each other no matter what goes on out there. My beautiful, cat-eyed, gorgeous sister is biracial, and she loves me to pieces. I have always loved her. She calls me her Miss Ebony, her fashion queen. We have always been close. But because of the differences in our skin color, people tended to gravitate toward her, and I was left home a lot. It always saddened her more than it did me when that happened.

Visualize the scene in the movie *The Color Purple* in which Nettie and her sister, Celie, were being torn apart from each other and were expressing their love by playing patty-cake even though they were being separated. I remember something so close to that scene with my sister. I teared up when I watched that movie. I would sometime beg my sister to go without me and not miss out on great opportunities to have fun and see new things. Every once in a while, I went with her, but I always felt very uncomfortable and like an outsider. Others would notice how I was treated differently, and I would feel bad for the person treating me like that, so I would try to straighten up as much as I could to not look like I knew what was really going on. My sister wasn't that flattered by being treated special.

Even as a girl, I was very sensitive and protective of other people's feelings even if it hurt me. That had to have been God directing my life. Sometimes, my sister would make sure I was included rather than excluded on purpose. Then she would play with only me at that time until the adult would say something about it, and we would interact for a short time. It was too much to keep up with, so I would purposely tell myself I didn't want to deal with the added wounds of rejection.

I didn't know why people were so mean, but that was what I was dealing with. I was sad, and I felt a false sense of responsibility. Clearly, my mother was not teaching that at home. We had to get along and agree to disagree. I was very quiet but very smart in school, and I made the honor roll many times. I was in the newspaper often for my successes. My mother and family were more excited than I was, of course, but I was an overachiever. I found it easy then to help others succeed and grow, but they would never give me credit for helping them.

Some would try to rekindle our relationship with an "I'm sorry," and I would gladly forgive them only for them to give me part two of the same treatment. I didn't want the credit for their success, but a thank-you would have been nice.

I have been a secret in many people's lives for one reason or another. That's okay to a certain extent, but in the spirit of usury, it's not. Romans 13:7a tells us to give honor to whom honor is due. It's natural for us to say thank you when someone helps us, period. But to get where you need to go and not acknowledge the help you received in getting there is not right. And then to act as if those who helped you succeed are strangers is even more wrong. That can hurt.

Once, a friend of mine helped someone get to a higher platform with an important introduction to the head man. The person she helped told her, "If you see me with them and we don't speak to you, don't take it personally." What kind of spirit is that? Help me, anybody!

That spirit of importance is a bad spirit; it's a prideful spirit, and prideful spirits always become humble spirits when they fall. And that's what happened to the person my friend helped. Pride goes before the fall. But today, those involved in that situation have matured and have moved on. I always like to end a story on a good note, and God is a good note! His mercy endures forever.

When I was hiding within myself, forming close relationships wasn't on the top of my list. I wanted to be genuinely friendly, and those who took the time to befriend me found out that that took just a minute. I would invite them into my personal space, no problem; my boundaries would drop. But people can lose respect for you after they cross over into your space; you find out they are just on assignment. The challenges of trust go up a notch.

But even being gifted, I would respect and allow people to be themselves even if I knew sometimes they had another agenda. I called it respect with tears. Sometimes, I wouldn't care to know until I walked it out. So it's not like I saw and knew everything. How sad would that be? But it's something to realize you've befriended the enemy in sheep's clothing after you take the time to pray and find out what's really going on.

Discover first of all if this is your trial to endure, because God has a way of working out things for the best even if at first glance His way looks a little insane. Not every road you take in life is your journey. The quicker you recognize that, the quicker you can get back on the correct road for you. You can rid yourself of fear in the light of truth, which will shine on all the devil's lies. If you stay in His Word and pray, God will lead you where He wants you to go. Some will try to take advantage of you and leave you high and dry, but you can get right back up and do it again because you love Jesus and do not allow fear to conquer you.

I never knew what was inside of me until it was challenged. Many times, fear would get the best of me due to my experiences growing up. I had to pray all the time to cast down fear. There were times when I felt I had no voice; that's how strong a grip fear had on me. Due to my being a gifted child and seeing spirits, fear controlled me most of my life until I faced it in a dream head-on. Hello fear! I had to take authority over the enemy that hated my very soul. I didn't have many people around who could explain to me how to deal with the spirit of fear. I had to rely on what I had learned, what worked for me, and use it until I knew for sure it was the Word of God in its entirety. You must stand on the Word of God to endure the tasks you face. The Holy Spirit and Jesus will work with you; the battle is already won. You go, girl!

Since then, I have met and shared my story about purpose and fear many times, which you will read about in some of my other books. It deals a lot with me having been born gifted and having seen spirits and dead people. But God set me free to use my gifts for His glory. We can be glorious if we declare His living Word. To Him be the glory for the things He has done! Thank you, Abba Father!

I thought I really lost my voice and could not speak at all at that point; I wasn't going to say anything, not a word. I used to practice humming just to see if I still had a voice. That might sound strange, but it is the truth.

Today, I use this part of my life to help others to handle difficult situations with their silence and to break through and open up doors inside. Many times, people wondered how I knew so much about being silent and full of fear in such detail. The Bible states that our lives are not our own; they have been bought with a price. Perfect love casts out fear. What you go through is for someone else. It's as if someone else is waiting for your completed trials and errors. You will find it stimulating to know how much we are designed to need each other. It is a team effort to complete and conquer the trials life presents us, good and bad. We can educate ourselves through each other's lives and live. This is called relationship, the thing we fear the most but love to have. Sometimes, I feel that my life is on display for everyone to see and point fingers at, only to register everything within me.

Life can be unfair at times, but it doesn't seem fair to be picked on or be humiliated by anyone. Often, it is as if I'm part of a life experiment. I can't remember volunteering my life to be on display as an example of truth and transparency for the world to decide who I might be or become. It is as if I had both hands stretched upward to God saying, "Choose me! Hey, God, over here!"

Somehow, I feel I'm moving through life in a fog that tends to cloud my mind with stressful thought of all kinds of what-ifs. I'm afraid to listen to the negative thoughts and lies of the adversary, and to say them aloud would create another type of fear. I didn't want to be in a fix where my thoughts and fears would contribute to others becoming contaminated and getting off-focus. I now know I was being hunted by perfection. I wanted everything to be perfect, orderly, and correct. I wanted the heart to do what was right and to be a righteous spirit. I fought dearly for what I felt was right, and so many times, I became a victim in my own war zone. It was me against the world, or so I thought.

I wanted to be perfect in all ways. I felt as if I were on a pedestal not by my own choosing to perform for a world that didn't care to know me for real. Later in life, I had to confront my perfection and realized I had a problem. I became my own subject. To my amazement, I wanted help!

I dealt with this spirit honestly, and it wasn't easy. The entrapment I built over my lifetime wasn't good enough when I realized I needed help. I finally couldn't see my way out of this crisis, and realized I built this mess myself—wow! When you think you're okay and find out you are screaming issues—oh my God, help me!

For the sake of righteousness, the more I built, the more I had to tear down. It wasn't the righteousness, it was what and whom I became in righteousness—private, isolated, distant, analytical, judgmental, secluded, the fixer and rescuer in the family—the list goes on. You lose yourself. It's your confession that makes you free, amen.

This is a wealth of information that will save your life if you could come face to face with yourself. Anger will try to set in while you are dealing with the truth. Fight or flight becomes a conscious choice.

You then vow to guard your heart, not consciously aware of the walls forming at the same time as life multiplies your pain and disappointments. So you try to live your whole life to keep up with the vows you made earlier in life as you become a doormat instead of a bridge for people to safely walk across. This is one of the most frightening things for any human being to go through. You make up your mind to deal with the truth and become helpless in a world you built for the sake of perfection. How sad is that? Many tears and prayers helped me erase the ravaging images of perfection and transform them into the gift of administration, which is much healthier and gives others a part to participate and build godly relationships. I had to reprogram my mind and take upon myself the new. I wanted God to help me download all the issues. I wanted to take upon the godly principles of the fruits of the spirits, which are love, joy, peace, patience, kindness, goodness, faithfulness, gentleness, and self-control (Galatians 5:22).

I couldn't take it anymore. My mind was tired, and my heart was heavy, and my spirit was disturbed, so I called out, "Help me, Lord!" How did I earn this position, especially so early in life? God said He knew me before I was in my mother's womb. Could He have chosen me for this? Surely not of myself! My life has always been somewhat of a mysterious adventure with many unplanned miracles and unheard of jobs and chores and stuff. Some things were completely made up on the spot to my knowledge.

I feel as if I were chosen to live completely on the edge with God. So occasionally, I let out the loudest and fearful cry for help wondering if anyone had heard me and would come to my rescue. But God would be the first to answer. I would thank Him so much for coming to my rescue. I would also ask at times, "Lord, can I have You with skin on? Someone here on earth whom I can touch, trust, and talk to without all the expectation of a perfect world? Until Your kingdom comes, I want to enjoy You in me here on earth."

That's when He began to connect me with other women who had similar or familiar cries. Sometimes, you need that relationship on earth to register what you're going through here on earth. This is Jesus with skin on. We need a safe place to cry out and be for real. It is a blessing to know when you cry, it can help someone else if you dare to become transparent. On that note, I started business and community outreach summits geared toward women's retreats and community summits. It exists today as HELP!, an organization that believes in reaching out to our community to touch and change lives for God through our business, talents, and strengths. We use our personal testimony and life challenges to reach women.

You have to be comfortable in your skin to tell your story. Let God position you in your shift. When Jesus was on the cross, He was in position to die for our sins. Even when we were out there doing our own thing, our destiny was on His mind. What love the Father has bestowed upon us that we might have the right to the tree of life! He did not come down off that cross. His position proved that love is greater when it's given away.

His story made history and helped position us to stay focused. We are to stay in position until we make His story our story, until Jesus gets the glory for our lives. Don't get off your post especially when everything seems wrecked. Don't miss your blessings. Don't let the enemy wear you out. You've come too far and have now passed go, so stand and fight to the end. "For I know the plans I have for you, declares the Lord, plans to prosper you and not to harm you, plans to give you hope and a future" (Jeremiah 29:11 NIV). The most beautiful part about Jesus on the cross is when He said, "My God, forgive them for they know not what they are doing." He committed His Spirit back to the Father. Mission accomplished.

Remember—stuff happens. You have to come out with your victory testimony. Let's get over the stuff and not fatten what belongs to the enemy. If you don't deal with that thing, the devil will weigh on you for that yolk to grow fat in your life. If you pay too much attention there, you will get stuck, and the enemy will continue adding more stuff to your stuff. Then you will be full of stuff. That's why you can't afford to stay stuck. You won't be able to find your way to being unstuck, and you'll be calling for help.

We always try to create a safe environment for women to be accountable to one another through their deepest hurts so they can recognize that their lives are not their own but are God's. We are our sisters' keepers. Everything we go through and confess builds trust and gives glory to God. Our kingdom focus is to see women healed and free to move totally in their God-given purpose. Healed women have a tendency to change the world through linking their pain.

When women become clearer about their God-given purposes, they reflect God's light in the world. There are many challenges just being a woman; when you add godly wife, mother, sister, and friend, you have all those shoes to fulfill. Yet still in all of it, God gets the glory right where you are in your season of life. Now try those shoes on for size. It's when you come to the place where enough is enough, women, that I salute you in your strength and your weakness and most of all your coming back. Staying in the fight and not giving in to society's dramatics in denying the call of being a real woman isn't an option as some might wish. God made us strong for a purpose. We can bend, stretch, and bear the pain of childbirth while getting back in shape for the next ball life rolls at us all in one breath if need be.

What we consider mistakes become God's mystery for help, God's hands stretched toward us to help us fulfill our purpose in life. I cried, and others heard me. They wanted to help me, and now they are being helped. Jesus is the answer for the world today; He is the only way. This is the hundredfold of blessings. The return on the blessing is peace and eternal life.

I believe in reaching out to you through my personal testimony and becoming transparent even though it might hurt me later. That's the chance I'm willing to take. Jesus laid His life down to save, change, and renew us.

I am choosing to lay my life down for my sisters in my testimony. I am gaining my identity and regaining my innocence. As I continue to write books, you will hear in the bloodlines the blood shed for my freedom of speech as I release the pains of life that patterned my walk of forgiveness.

It is easier to forgive others. The fight is forgiving yourself, right? That is working itself out through God's true love along with the love of my family. The lies of the enemy cease.

Thank you, Jesus, for loving me and being able to experience the real love of God before leaving this earth. My prayers are that not one person leaves earth without being touched by the real love of God.

God is the repairer of the breach and healer of the land, the Prince of our peace of mind. God, help me to heal everything life presents. One woman's cry is another woman's answer. The end is a new beginning. It is finished. Enough is enough. The blood of Jesus paid for our sins and returned us to the Father.

Chapter 3

The End
—to a New Beginning

Jesus hung on the cross in victory for our souls to return to the Father. He's our creator and Lord of Lords. He reigns forevermore! Alpha and Omega and the in-between!

"Father, forgive them; for they know not what they do" (Luke 23:34 KJV) is an unselfish prayer. The first thing to learn from these words is Jesus's love for those responsible for crucifying Him. He paid a debt. His final words were "It is finished" (John 19:30 NIV). Jesus called out with a loud voice, "Father, into thy hands I commit my spirit. When He had said this, He breathed His last" (Luke 23:46 NIV). Because of Jesus's sacrifice on the cross, we have a second chance at life. Thank God! The end to a new beginning, therefore, doesn't mean quitting. That's what the devil will tell you.

You must recognize your worth through all that you've gone through. It is truly worth all Jesus died for on the cross. He rose to prove He is the the great I Am, the Alpha and Omega, the Beginning and the End!

Chapter 4

One Woman's Cry Is Another Woman's Answer —Your Story for His Glory

Everything God made is good. Raise your head, grab your identity in the risen Christ, and live. You beat the enemy when you tell your story and create your history in Christ, who brings good news. When you don't know who you are, the enemy can easily get the upper hand until you shut it down. Your life, your time, is precious. Let no one rob you of it. It took me some time to recognize that was one of my issues. *No* became a popular and kind word for me when I said it under the anointing.

Your life is your life, and your time is your time. How much of your life and time do you spend on the things of God? Your life experiences wrapped in the palm of His hand can give hope to others.

Let there be light, and let it shine bright on you! I couldn't imagine how God would use my mess for His message. To my amazement, as I share my issues in life, that could easily have been a total setback. The weird thing about it is that my personality fits in perfectly with Christ's designer cleanup. The fear of stepping out the first time to tell my story a little at a time shocked me, but Jesus covered me from the shame of it, and His grace laced with love saw me through. People told me afterward how my testimony had blessed them. Some identified with what had happened to me and said one day that they would be bold enough to share their stories. I still hear this a lot. It became easier, and it continues to help others. Men too come forth to identify with pain, share their experiences, and move on after being healed. Wow!

Let's begin with the testimonies of some women who have cried out. If you are in one of these positions, this is your chance to begin progressing toward your destiny and purpose.

Please use this book and testimonies here to be inspired by God, who loves you. Do not believe the lies of the deceiver, who has already been defeated by Jesus's blood of Jesus. You are a winner; you are victorious in the Lord already.

The stories you are about to read are true stories; these women have opened up their lives to you and for you. I hope you will choose to share your stories with HELP! Pain is as real as the weight it carries. With the Lord's help, you can be free forever! Your test is now your testimony of war against the enemy! Remember—one woman's cry is another woman's answer.

Much prayer has gone forth and does so today for those who have given us permission to share their stories with others and bring them hope. We ask that you keep each woman in prayer. With the Lord's help, each woman has been transparent about her encounter with pain.

Pain is real. It doesn't matter whether we are young or old—we all have been touched by it. It can be identified by the hurt it carries. Pain can have a deadly sting. It can hold you hostage and rob you of a good life and relationships. The bolder you are in confronting and addressing it, the quicker you will recover from it. With the help of the Lord, the true healer and physician who knows you inside out, you can be victorious over pain, and He will get the glory. The blood of Jesus cleanses all hurts and pain and thereby shames the enemy.

I think about the Lord and what He's done for me. My soul shouts out, "Hallelujah! Thank You, Lord, for saving me." I was on my way to hell for real, but before I hit bottom, I realized it wasn't a place I wanted to be. I cried out for real, "Lord, save me!" I had so much hatred in me on the way to hell that I wanted to die, but Jesus lifted me up and showered me with His pure love. I never wanted to get anywhere near hell again. God gave me choices—life over death, heaven over hell, love over hate. What marvelous love He has for us!

Chapter 5

Keeping It Real! It's My Confession —A Prophet's Daughter

Keep it real. Do we really know what that means? Most people think it's just a saying, but I think keeping it real means being honest with yourself no matter how hard that can be. Staying true to who you are and what you believe in will be its own reward. Although everyone may not agree with you, that does not matter. In the Bible, God said, "You shall know the truth and the truth shall make you free." There is a freedom in being real.

It is a freedom for you and for those around you to see I am as real as they get. What you see is what you get with me. I am the same every day. You may have an image you're trying to portray to those around you. Step back and look at yourself. Do you see how hard it is to get up each day and act in a way that really isn't you?

We're entering a time when there will be great confusion in the world. People will not know whom to trust. They will not know right from wrong or good from evil. So it will be very important to stay true to yourself no matter what life throws at you. I know it is easier said than done, but you have to keep it real.

Keep it real with your kids, pastors, friends, and family. People deep down really want honesty. Most of all, you must keep it real with yourself.

As you let people influence what you do or who you are, more and more of you is lost to the lie each day. Then before you know it, your true self no longer exists! Some people believe the lies and find themselves in a mess, but the Word says that the truth shall make you free, not a half-truth or what others say is the truth! People look all through the lies for happiness, but they will never find peace and identity in lies. The lies spoken about you and the words of hate spoken to you can rob you of your true identity. Hey, maybe you can get back some of your ways, but if you lose yourself, you will never be that person again.

I was the firstborn and the only girl. I have two younger brothers. My parents are very respected in our home, church, and communities, my mom especially. As a little girl, I came to realize that growing up a prophet's daughter was very demanding. I found myself always being prejudged just because of who my mother was. Many young women would try to take up all my mom's time. I never understood why they wanted my brothers and me to call them our sisters. Even at that young age, I knew they wanted to have our mom. I did not mind then. I knew that no one could take my place.

My family eventually moved to Canada for a short time, and from there, we moved to a small town in Texas that had very few black people. I hated it! I started to act out, which did not last too long, because we found a church that we really liked and got involved in. As time went on, I fell in love with this small town. I had a group of best friends, and we kept each other in line. I was home again. My family lived in that town till I was in the ninth grade. At the beginning of my high school years, we moved to a Dallas suburb.

Because we moved a few times during those years, it was hard for me to make good friends, and every high school girl wants a best friend. My last two years of high school were spent in a city about thirty minutes outside Dallas. I became close to one girl. I wanted to fit in, so I did whatever she did, and I got into some trouble from time to time during that season of my life. Because of the choices I made, I found myself in situations that I should not have been in. I have been hurt by those closest to me and was abused by others.

I am not where I should be, but I respect God, and I see His hand of grace in my life. In spite of the bad choices I have made, God has been good to me. God blessed me with my sons. Being a single mom of two boys has been one of my greatest joys. I know that one day, they will grow up to be wonderful men.

My Summary

Being a preacher's kid is not always easy. Many times, you fight uphill battles with all eyes on you. Every time your name is mentioned, the room becomes silent; everyone wants to hear bad news about you. There's no place to hide; you are expected to do good always. Now what kind of life is that? Is it fair?

Some people are judgmental of everyone except those in their families; that's when everything becomes hush-hush. Violence is silence, and fear is in control of the lives that bear their pain.

Ministers' children are not exempt from the pain of life. The call on their families to serve the Lord puts them in a brighter light for more eyes to see God working through them. They are chosen for the task, and failure plays a major part of the lessons learned. It's a stool that lifts you up with hope, but you can still fall off it, fail, and suffer pain.

When you get back up again, keep marching forward until you get your next orders from the Lord. As you step up into greatness and testify to the glory of God, He will shine the light for you to see your way out of the enemy's entrapments. You will realize every ball thrown your way isn't always to be caught, but you need to see them because God meant them to be in the season you are in.

God gives us all time as a gift. What you do with your time is documented by the best timekeeper, the ultimate judge who never misses a case. Define your time on purpose. Find out who God is and you will know who you are. Life will look a lot brighter from where you are sitting. Arise and claim your inheritance. God loves preachers' kids, and He understands your life and will help you.

As you read her story, maybe you can identify with her pain and agony of betrayal and quick decisions that led her to rebel. But God is faithful through it all and in all who seek Him for the truth. Keeping it real is required if you want to be promoted in the body of Christ. The sooner you deal with all of you, the quicker you can move forward. It may not be what you always want to hear, it may not always be a feel-good message, but it will be real.

As ministers, we pray over our family for God's protection that He will encamp the angels around about us and keep hurt, harm, and any evil far away from them in Jesus's name.

Many times, the families you see on the church's fans used to cool off aren't the family in the pulpit. Several of them come together only for a photo, and someone tells them to smile. Is that real or not?

When I look at those families and see how cute and together they look, I wish our family was like that until reality kicks in. It takes God's love to create a beautiful family portrait. A family is as real as the choices its members make. Let God be the judge; don't worry about others' negative opinions of the people. Make good choices and know that God loves you. You will greet the people you meet, and you will meet the people you greet.

Enjoy the present as you anticipate your future; it's all good! Jeremiah 12:3a tells us, "But Thou, O Lord, knows me: Thou hast seen me, and tried mine heart toward Thee."

Chapter 6

The Purple Heart
—God! Please Help Me!

I believe that we all have life stories that have made us who we are. Our stories' beginnings affect how they end.

Some people's stories are full of lies and deception. Others' stories are about how they finally met that one person they could spend the rest of their lives with. My story is a story in itself.

I was born in Arkansas. My father was a very quiet man. My mother had a lot to say; she had a mind of her own. They worked hard to keep a roof over our heads at the ages of sixteen and seventeen. They struggled, but no matter how hard it got, they never gave up. My parents always sacrificed for me. When I was about a year and a half, we ran out of my milk during a snowstorm that made travel from our home on a mountain difficult. Regardless, my father walked down that mountain to a store six miles away for my milk. My mom had to work and go to school at the same time. When she needed to work, she just carried me along. Those are the kind of parents I have.

When I was about two and a half, my parents had my little brother. We were best friends from the start. We ate, laughed, cried, and got in trouble together. We were each other's best friends.

I was a very talkative and outgoing child all throughout school. Junior high was tough. I never felt good; I was always tired. I felt that I never got any sleep though I was sleeping nine hours a night. During eighth grade, I kept getting sicker; I could not handle the cold or heat well. I had a 104-degree fever for five days straight. It broke, but then it came right back full force. I couldn't move without feeling horrible pain. It felt as if electricity was running through my legs and arms. At times, Dad had to carry me from the car to the couch.

At night, I would get stuck in my bed unable to move. I remember having to go to the restroom, but no one could hear me, so I would just lie there till Dad got up in the morning. I was in and out of it most of the time. Many times, Mom would wake up in the middle of the night and walk through the living room. I would cry out to her and ask her to please pray for my legs, and she would. The Holy Spirit would have to help ease the pain because nothing we tried would work. I kept having dreams of dying. I would call Mrs. Rosemary and tell her about my dreams of death, crosses, and cemeteries. She would pray that my parents and I would find out what was wrong with me. No one knew, and they certainly couldn't comfort me.

I remember crying out to God, "What is happening to me?" The doctors knew something was slowly killing me, but they did not know what it was. Thinking that I was dying but not knowing from what was one of the hardest and scariest things I ever went through.

I prayed that God would show us what was killing me. He answered my prayer not long after that. I remember the day as if it were yesterday. My dad and mom picked me up from school, which was very unusual. They waited until I got to the car, and my mom said, "They know what is wrong with you, but they will not tell us what it is until we get to the hospital, and they want to start treatment as soon as possible."

I felt relieved but fearful at the same time. When we arrived, the doctors told us that I had lupus. "You are very lucky we finally figured it out," they said, "because you could have died by age sixteen." I was scared. I wondered what the next step would be. I went through many treatments to get the disease under control. Things really started to get better for me but only by the grace of God.

You never appreciate your life till it's almost taken from you. I was doing so much better by age sixteen. Now, I'm an adult and am enjoying every minute of it! I thank my family, who supported, comforted, and believed in me and my God, who spared my life. What more could I ever ask for?

Being part of The Green Rose Ministries has been one of the greatest opportunities I have had for healing. I have never left the retreat the same.

My Summary

I remember meeting this young woman and her mother when she was seven. I had met her uncle through a mutual friend; he introduced me to her mother, and we ended up in a late-night visit. I didn't realize the relationship would go as far as it did. Sometimes, you meet some people and that's all it is. But we grew fond of each other, and we knew it was a God relationship from then on. Our questions and answers were fitting together perfectly. Our time was always running into another day.

When I realized this young girl needed healing, it shocked us all. She told me about her dreams of death and cemeteries; her nightmares victimized her. We prayed and fasted and believed God would reveal why she was in so much pain. The doctors conducted all kinds of tests, but nothing showed up. They told her parents that perhaps she was trying to get special attention by expressing her fears for her parents. She always feared something was going to happen to them, and of course we prayed against that and constantly tried to comfort her until she had the next dream or pain. I always knew God had a calling on her life because the enemy fought her a lot.

She loved God so much, and she had a prayer life at an early age. Her faith always stood out to me, especially when we would pray together. We have witnessed many miracles of healing in her and her family's lives; they were challenges, but they also became successes.

After her lupus diagnosis and her treatment, we believe God will completely heal her and free her and her family from suffering.

She thanks God for healing her, and I will never stop believing that God will completely heal her of lupus in Jesus's name. God is good all the time!

Chapter 7

How Pain Dared Me to Dream!
—Fear! Rejection! Abandonment! Me?

We all have a story to tell. We all can relate to pain. But despite all that has happened in my life, I trust God. No matter my troubles or my pain, I challenge myself to take courage and face them. This is my story.

I woke up in the middle of the night in a hospital bed. It was dark and cold, and I couldn't get comfortable. The woman in the bed next to me was snoring. I didn't know where I was or how I had gotten there. I got out of the bed and looked outside. I saw a long hallway with a desk at the end of it. I heard faint voices. I walked down the hall to the nurses' station and asked if I could call my mom. They told me I had to wait until the next day during the designated time.

I told them I was cold, so they gave me a pair of sweat pants I could barely fit into, but they made me warmer. I fell asleep and woke up three hours later to the voice of one of the nurses who wanted me to take some pills. I wondered what they were for.

I was able to call my mom at two o'clock. She was excited to hear from me because I had been asleep for two weeks. She didn't know where I was. She knew only that the ambulance took me to the hospital. I had been transported to two different hospitals. She made sure I gave her the address for her to bring me some clothes. The nurses informed me that visits were on certain days for only a short time.

My roommate was a heavyset woman with elephantiasis. I would lotion her legs and help her around the room. She felt that I was an angel because of the service I showed her.

A couple of days went by before my mom visited me. I was so overmedicated that I couldn't even think straight. I remember trying to show her something outside and running right into a glass door. My medication was muddling my brain. I was frustrated. I wanted to go home. My mom comforted me and encouraged me; she said I would be okay. She helped me cope.

But I felt trapped in the hospital. I wanted to go home. I made two escape attempts. The first one was when I was scheduled to go to court. My roommate told me that when they took me to the van, I was to run and scream for a guy she knew. When the officers took me to the van, I was barefoot with sweat pants and a T-shirt. I took off running into a field, and an officer was on my heels. I ran as fast as I could until I reached a gas station. I screamed for help.

I remember grabbing onto the back of a man's truck with all my medical files I was supposed to present at court. The files scattered when the officer grabbed me. He threw me against the truck, handcuffed me, and walked me back across the field. I felt stabbing pressure on the bottom of my feet from walking slowly on the stick-filled grass. When I got back to the van, they put shackles on my feet. After that incident, I knew I was going to be in the hospital for a little while.

The second escape attempt was more dramatic. I was so frustrated about being bound up in that place. I was surrounded by strangers with their own issues. Every twenty minutes, I would go outside into a fenced-in area with the smokers on their smoke breaks just to get fresh air. At night, I would look at the stars and think of my goals and dreams of being successful. I wondered how I could finish school if I was trapped in that place.

One night after a smoke break, I ran to the nurses' station when the visitors were about to depart. I jumped on the counter and tried to get out. The security officers grabbed me, the nurses came over, and they worked as a team to sedate me. They put me in an isolation cell. I rolled up into a ball and cried myself to sleep.

When I woke up, I called my mom to tell her what had happened. I was angry. She shared with me how I should stop trying to escape because that would keep me there longer. My mom prayed with me, and I felt much better after our conversation. She encouraged me to read my Bible and pray.

After that, I was determined to overcome my situation. I began to pray and read scriptures. God began to help me to embrace what I was going through even though I didn't understand it. The doctors and nurses diagnosed me with a condition I didn't even have. I had symptoms of it, but it was only because I had overwhelming stress in my life. I spent two months in the hospital.

I finally was released after my mom fought to get me out of there. When I returned home, it was difficult to return to daily life. I returned to school, but I could barely process my thoughts because of the medication they were giving me. I would lie in bed all day because I had no energy. I lost all motivation to live. One day, I cried out to God from the depth of my heart, "God, I feel like I am dying spiritually, mentally, emotionally, and physically. I need You to help me live. I want to dream again."

I had officially hit rock bottom. I was so used to setting goals and dreams five years at a time. I was an honor student in school, but there I was unable to even think. I slowly began to have hope when I decided that I should stop taking the medication they prescribed for me.

I shared with my mom my decision, and she supported me. People would talk about me, stare at me, and even gossip about me. They saw that I was different from before but didn't know what I had gone through. I felt judged, ridiculed, hated, and rejected, but I found comfort in the fact that God loved me with an everlasting love and had a plan for my life.

I revisited my dreams of finishing school and doing what I loved for the rest of my life—serving people. I reenrolled in school. I struggled getting the grades I was used to getting. My comprehension, understanding, and focus were lacking; I believed that was because of the drugs. I'd fall asleep as I was working on my homework. I fought through the difficulties and pressed on with the help of the Lord. I began to read a little more each day.

I prayed and trusted God. He slowly helped me to think again. I finished school and managed to graduate with honors.

Despite life's obstacles, I always dared to dream. I had every reason to quit. I lost my ability to think, I was viewed as disabled and incapable, and most people lost hope in me. Growing up in a Christian home, I always had a praying mother who didn't give up on me. She was by my side as a constant support. I am thankful I experienced the struggle of my situation because it taught me to stay humble.

I am now living my dreams. Never despise the difficulties that come your way. I shared my story to give you hope. I was in the hospital because I had overexerted myself. I was angry and felt rejected and abandoned. My friends and some of my family treated me as an outcast. The pain and hurt I experienced was so deep that I couldn't face certain people for a while. I had to learn to forgive. People who respected me in the past no longer respected me because of what I had gone through. They judged me without understanding the truth about what happened to me. God has helped me over the years to overcome the pain. Will you dare to dream again?

My Summary

You never know what others go through until you hear their true stories. We all have stories, but we all have to choose to tell them.

This beautiful woman shared her story because she knew it would help others who were in pain and were stressed out and angered by their problems and situations. Telling your story and hearing others' stories will stir up the truth and help everyone break the silence and fear that can haunt them. Proverbs 11:14 (KJV) tells us, "Where no counsel is, the people fall: but in the multitude of counsellors there is safety." Proverbs 11:14 (NLV) says, "A nation falls where there is no wise leading, but it is safe where there are many wise men who know what to do."

Do not go down any path that leads to self-destruction. You can medicate your pain, but that will not erase it; pain will affect your health. You will be medicated to the point of numbness until you need the medication again, but ultimately, you will become tired of suffering and want to deal with reality.

Constant pain became a way of life for her. Tunneling through life can unravel much pain inside of the biggest hurts. If it weren't for the Lord being on this woman's side, where would she be now? The vicious cycle of life caused her pain to fester and grow and gave her thoughts of death. But God turned her life around for His glory!

Sometimes, we need to allow God to take charge, but that can be hard for us to do. We don't have to fight for His love because He gives it freely.

I would love to know that every human has experienced true love before leaving this world. The way things look today, that seems impossible, but God can make the impossible possible!

To see her come face to face with her emotions amazed me. She chose to deal with her pain and face her challenges. Unlock your purpose, and help somebody unselfishly. God got you!

This wonderful woman's testimony has helped many others in leadership positions and in her community and life. Watching her over the years grow is amazing to witness; she reaches out with God's help. Love the Word of God. Jesus is truly her refuge, and she knows it.

I thank her for sharing her story. Look at what we are up against in our society as far as health and people being misdiagnosed are concerned. But God can handle your pain when doctors can't explain it. Help is on the way! I know for sure you don't have stay locked up.

Woman, God Wants You Healed! is another book I have written that will soon be on the market. God loves you. Jesus is the way. The Holy Spirit will lead and direct you into all truth. "Ask and it will be given to you; Seek and you will find; Knock and the door will be opened to you" (Matthew 7:7 NIV).

This woman is a blessing to others whom she helps with health issues. What the devil meant for harm, God turned it around for His glory!

Chapter 8

Oh No! I Can't Remember!
—God! Pease, Not My Mind!

On New Year's Eve in 1975, my six-year-old daughter and I went with my boyfriend to a friend's house for a get-together to eat and get high. We wanted to celebrate before going out that night for a big party at a cabaret. On the way home, we were in a terrible car accident. I woke up in the hospital, looked around, and started crying. I was thinking I had missed the New Year's Eve dance. *What happened? Why am I here?* I asked myself. My head was bandaged. I pushed the button to call the nurse in, and I started screaming. They gave me a sedative.

When I woke up again, I asked them what had happened. They told me I had been in a car accident. I didn't remember that. I remembered missing the New Year's Eve dance, but that was it. I had cracked my skull open in the accident. The brain tissue that was exposed was the part of the brain that handled memory. The doctors told my mom that they should look for a nursing home for me because I wouldn't be able to take care of myself. I would become a vegetable.

I might remember some things, but the type of injury I had suffered would prevent me from thinking and operating as normal. People who visited me told me who they were, but I did not recognize them. One woman asked if I knew her, and I said, "Yes. You are a friend of my mom's, Odessa." She started crying and said, "Yes, I'm Odessa."

Later, I found out she was my mom. My sister came to see me, but I didn't know her either. My boyfriend came to see me. His mouth was wired up, and he was on crutches, I didn't know him either. I did recognize some people from work, however. The doctor said I would remember people or events I had good memories about.

After I was in the hospital awhile, they said I was going home to stay with Odessa. When I walked into the house, I saw a picture of my daughter and me. I said, "Oh no! Where is my daughter? How come nobody told me?" I started crying and screaming, "Where is she? Is she dead?" My mind started racing. Why hadn't anyone told me? Why didn't I remember?

They called the doctor, gave me a pill, and told me to lie down. They told me my daughter was at a children's orthopedic hospital. They said I would see her later. I asked them why I didn't remember my daughter.

That night, I got on my knees and prayed, "God, help me! I didn't even know I had a daughter. I remember hearing my mom say pray and believe in God. God, I am praying to You now. I know I haven't prayed to You since I was little, but I need my memory back. I don't even know who I am. What else don't I know that I should? God, I need You to help me!" I cried for a long time on my knees.

They took me to see my daughter, who had undergone surgery. She would need more as she got older, I was told. I went to a physiologist and psychiatrist the next day; they had me look at pictures and words. I went to see a lawyer as well. This continued for a few weeks.

One day, I asked the doctor when I could go back to work. I was tired of staying in my room, taking pills six times a day, staying in bed, and not watching TV. I was bored stiff. The physiologist and psychiatrist said that I was doing much better than they had expected. They let me go back to work part time.

I started working two hours a day, and then four, and then six until I was up to eight. The specialists could not believe I had recovered so well. The specialists have it documented that God must have done something miraculous. They had no other explanation for my recovery. My mom did not have to find a nursing home for me. I was healed and still am healed, praise the Lord!

Over twenty-five years ago, I was saved and filled with the Holy Ghost at the Seed of Abraham Pentecostal Church. The Lord delivered me from sin, and I praise Him for that. I finally understood about Jesus Christ, God's Son and the blood He shed for me, and the awesome power of the Holy Spirit.

Having responded to the call of God to Christian ministry and having satisfied all the biblical requirements, I was ordained on July 1, 2001. On occasion, I went to a youth center and a women's shelter to minister and pray for the youth and women who were incarcerated.

In November 2007, prophetess and overseer Rosemary Green asked me to be part of the staff for The Green Rose Ministries as Minister of HELP! as head intercessor. I am honored to be in this position. HELP! is God's work; what more can I say?

Since attending the Green Rose Retreat in January 2008 in Texas where Rosemary Green was the hostess, I have never been the same. We got together and heard Prophetess Rosemary say, "The Lord said this is a setup!" We all went off praising the Lord, crying, dancing, speaking in unknown tongues, running, and screaming. All we had gone through just to get there was a miracle, a trial. We went through many storms and hardships just to make it there. God did show up, and I have not been the same. God gave us an impartation. He blessed us so much that words cannot explain it. I know we were supposed to be there and receive something precious from God.

The Green Rose Ministries have helped me step far out on faith to a place where I have never been. My whole walk has been by faith, and it still is. I have experienced the Holy Spirit in a different way. I shut myself in with Him, ask questions about my life, and request His instructions for me. He is faithful to His Word!

The Green Rose Ministries experience has moved me to a new level in Christ I never want to leave. I'm working with The Green Rose Ministries to be trained, motivated, inspired, prayed for, corrected, and ministered to. I expect to experience more of the power and authority of God so I can use what God has given me to a greater degree—as we have heard many times, higher heights and deeper depths. New levels and new devils, and guess what? We will win! I will not move, say, or do anything without instructions from Him in prayer. I would never have been in the place I am now if Prophetess Rosemary had not been in tune with the Holy Spirit to come see about me when she did. Now, we are in tune with each other, but then, I was totally broken and hurt and disappointed in my so-called friends.

I needed God to deliver me, so God sent Prophetess Rosemary to walk me through it all. I love my sister and appreciate her for being there at the appointed time. The Lord healed me and gave me my life back. All the glory goes to you, Lord!

My Summary

This woman of God came into my life at a time when I needed a true friend and sister. Understanding and prayer came with the relationship. God sent her especially to me. God loves me. The odds were against me many times. I couldn't identify the unspoken battles I fought out of pure jealousy and envy that I hadn't caused and had caused me years of agony. I needed an outside view of the pictures that were being framed around me. God sent her and her sweet and dear sister, who has gone on to be with the Lord. The Lord knew I needed a friend who would respect me but rebuke me when needed, and she was that person for me as I am for her. The relationship came with the accountability and honor I had prayed for. Being misunderstood is not cool, and being lied about isn't popular. To have a friend and witness who is objective and uncompromising in her relationship with God and me is very rare.

When I found out what she had gone through way before I had met her, that showed me God loved her and was still in the healing business. He is an awesome God!

I knew you would be blessed to hear her miraculous testimony. What a mighty God we serve! He's real and ready! Isaiah 59:1 (KJV) states, "Behold the Lord's hand is not shortened, that it cannot save; neither His ear heavy, that it cannot hear." He Got You!

How frustrating it can be for someone who has lost his or her memory. I can't imagine not knowing my own child, family, and others. Your past is erased, and you are lost in the present. Your future is waiting for you to catch up. You are surrounded by strangers. You hope your memory returns so you can make sense of everything. I marvel at God's creation, His beautiful handiwork. In 1 Corinthians 2:16b (KJV), we read, "But we have the mind of Christ."

God will help you remember the important things if you rest in His arms. God is good, and He is here for you right now. Give Him glory for things He has done for you. He is Lord, and He cares for you. He wants to HELP! you with whatever problems you have; if it bothers you, it bothers Him. Psalm 18:6 (KJV) states, "In my distress I called upon the Lord; and cried unto my God: He heard my voice out of His temple, and my cry came before Him, even unto His ears."

John 14:26 KJV: "But the Comforter, which is the Holy Spirit, whom the Father will send in My Name, He will teach you all things, and bring ALL things to your remembrance, whatsoever I have said unto you."

Psalm 71:1 KJV: "In Thee, O Lord, do I put my trust; let me never be put to confusion."

Psalm 71:8 KJV: "Let my mouth be filled with thy praise and with thy honor all the day."

Romans 12:2b KJV: "But be ye transformed by the renewing of your mind, that you may prove what is that good, and executable, and perfect, will of God."

Ephesians 4:23 KJV: "And be renewed in the spirit of your mind."

2 Timothy 1:12b KJV: "For I know Whom I have believed, and am persuaded that He is able to keep that which I have committed unto Him against that Day."

Hebrews 2:1 KJV: "Therefore we ought to give the more earnest heed to the things which we have heard, lest at anytime we should let them slip."

God blessed my friend with a full recovery, and now, she's in a prophetic ministry serving God! The Lord will restore your mind because He wants you to use it for His glory!

Chapter 9

My Childhood Abuser —Must I Forgive Him?

Several years ago, the Lord began to deal with me about forgiving my childhood abuser. With all the hatred and bitterness I held in my heart, it was next to impossible to hear Him and be used by Him. I battled depression and fears every day of my life. The effects of the abuse filtered into other parts of my life. For instance, I would watch certain movies that had a sexual abuse content, and this rage would just pour out of me. I would scream and cry and yell at anyone who came into the room during those times.

My husband was so patient with me even when he was on the receiving end of my hatred and anger. When I wanted to run because of shame, his response was "That's not the answer," as he called me by my name. I hated how I treated my family. I began to cry out to God to help me forgive my abuser.

I would go through times when I thought I had forgiven him, but I eventually figured out that it was not true forgiveness, it was just due to the emotional roller-coaster I was on. I started to talk to my pastor, and his wife, and Mrs. Rosemary because I was so desperate for an answer to the pain. My pastor would have an altar call, and I would be the first one down there!

Every time I showed up there, he would lead me through the forgiveness prayer. I kept waiting for that peace that said all was finally well. That went on for about six weeks until I got so angry with God that I just let it all out. I told Him I did not want to forgive my abuser. "Why is he going to get away with what he did to me? Where were You when all that was happening to me? It isn't fair what You're asking me to do!" You get the point.

I ended my yelling with tears of surrender. I said, "God, I don't want to forgive this man, but out of obedience to Your Word, I choose to forgive him. God, You will have to work forgiveness into my heart because I do not have it to give him!" It was then that I felt a sense of relief and peace. That was not what I was expecting to happen, especially after how I had just talked to my Lord. I wondered for a long time why God never struck me dead after the way I yelled at Him.

Then one day, he gave me a scripture. Isaiah 43:25–26 (LASB) states, "I, even I, who blots out your transgressions for my own sake and remember your sins no more. Review the past for me, let us urge the matter together, state the case for your innocence." Wow!

I still thought about my situation sometimes several times a day, but the key to it was saying, "I choose to forgive you." I did not feel it at all the first 500 times I said it, however. But as time went on, I thought less and less about all that I had gone through as a child, and six months later as I was walking away from someone who wanted to know my story, I realized for the first time that I was not as angry anymore. I was shocked at how God had worked all that out without my help! I just surrendered it back to Him repeatedly until I let it go all the way.

Although that was nine years ago, I still thank God for what He did for me and my family. I know without a shadow of doubt that He truly does mend broken hearts.

My Summary

Listening to this young woman's story takes me aback. She wanted to know everything about the things of God today. Without knowing what she was requesting, we started our journey.

We stayed up all night at our first meeting. Her questions were intense; I knew she was a prime candidate for a real touch from God. And with me, there were no hard questions, even when she thought there were. I wasn't thrown off by her anger when it surfaced even though I didn't quite understand it all. But with God's help and guidance, I learned a lot.

The Lord is truly a teacher if you desire to be taught. I loved her hunger for the truth. I remembered her challenge for me was to take her on as a friend and later as a mentor. I love challenges, especially from God. At times, I asked her to write down her feeling to get them out as a form of confession. From this, memories and dreams would arise, and as they did, we dealt with them head-on until the pain disappeared and God healed it.

The first time she brought me her journal, it appeared to be chicken scratchings. I asked her about all the deep, dark scratches on that paper. She said she had nothing to say other than she was storming mad and it felt good to mark up the pages. She said she would cry. So we visited the pain it brought on right then and there. Of course, God showed up again and healed her. The more open you are with your stuff, the quicker the Lord can heal you. Letting go of it is the key. I'm not saying that won't be a challenge, but it comes down to how badly you want to be free.

Our relationship grew quickly because of where we were and where we were going. We were excited that the Lord was answering her prayers and easing her pain. It was like revisiting a crime scene at times when we addressed her pain and shame. But prayer brought on change. She felt joy and happiness as she released the truth and exposed the lies. When she would write in her journal, her memory and clips of dreams surfaced. She and I would talk on the phone until late at night. She went through more deliverance, as needed. She wanted to be free. Her family witnessed the changes in her. Thank God she had an understanding husband and a caring family. I'm honored by their gifts of giving.

She hungered to know and embrace God and His healing. She was able to confront her abuser. They met at a park with their spouses, and he asked her for forgiveness. She forgave him gladly after years of true healing. She embraced him for the first time without the yuck, and they were okay. She wanted to be free so she could move on with her life. You have to want to be healed and free very badly, but then, you can share your healing and freedom with others who are crying out for help, especially those who are dealing with similar situations. Pain is pain!

Forgiveness is a gift you give to another. Be ready to forgive over and over. Matthew 18:21–22 (KJV) states, "Then came Peter to Him, and said, Lord. How oft shall my brothers against me, and I forgive him? Till seven? Jesus saith unto him, I say not unto thee, Until seven times: but, Until seventy times seven. The Mystery of forgiveness is you become Free! The root of forgiveness is Love."

> 1 John 4:8b KJV: "God is Love."
>
> 1 John 4:9 KJV: "In this was manifested the love of God. God sent His Son into the world, that we might live through Him."
>
> 1 John 3:1a KJV: "What manner of love the Father hath bestowed upon us, that we be called the sons of God. You belong to Him. You are in His image. You are loved."
>
> Numbers 14:18a KJV: "The Lord is long-suffering, and great mercy. Forgiving you for your iniquities and transgressions when you truly repents. How wonderful it is to serve an awesome God! He loves us unconditionally and for that I am grateful."
>
> Hebrews 2:1 KJV: "Therefore we ought to give the more earnest heed to the things which we have heard, lest at anytime we should let them slip."

Chapter 10

Their Stories' Endings Are Your Beginnings —End the Pain That You Carry

Thank you for getting to this point in my book. I hope you reread these stories if you need a point of reference when you are dealing with your pain.

Remember that you're not the only one in pain. Pain has many names and faces, but it is real. You can't just pick one person out without you in; it doesn't work that way. Your pain and hurt can help others in many ways. If you've been delivered, it's time to share your testimony and pass the big test of pride and shame.

I'm not saying you should set yourself up to be hurt, but when the opportunity presents itself and it's safe to do so, help others. That will help you to overcome the war in your mind! Cast it down. Revelation 12:11a (KJV) states, "And they overcame him by the blood of the Lamb and by the words of their testimony." You have two powerful weapons of spiritual destruction in action in this scripture—the blood of the Lamb and your testimony as a believer of His Word. It is written that you are an overcomer!

God, who loves you dearly, will heal your wounds. We are all His daughters and sons. Isn't that good news?

Pain is real, but we serve a God who carried it, and we won through His sacrifice. If you feel you are called to help women who are hurting, do your best to help them as led by God and not by manipulation. Pray! Pray! Pray!

My Summary

Now that you've heard our stories, think about the story you could share. God will lead you to when, how, and what to do with it. Don't think doing so will be easy, but it will be easier than taking your story to the grave.

The truth about yourself exposes your vulnerability to others and can leave you feeling naked and ashamed. This is the reason to be open to godly counsel that will require you to be accountable and transparent. Free people free people, but hurt people hurt people.

Many of our experiences direct or redirect our lives. There we are, driven to many perception and precautions, as we take off our masks and travel into life. Some might listen to these stories or yours and say that did not happened that way. They might even have evidence not known to you that can perhaps change your story in some way. So until that's revealed to you, your own perceptions can cause you pain. For how many years has your pain directed your life? You've moved, married, had children, and stayed away from things and people in survival mode until you received healing if you did.

You put yourself on lockdown to not register the pain it caused you all these months and years. Are you responsible for what you don't know? No! I've had several perceptions in life that I could have promised took place as far as I could remember, and years went by, and I made some major decision to avoid being hurt. Then later in life, it was brought to my attention, and I had to look at it from another prospective and make more sense of why it happened.

A truthful answer to your story can expose the lies and allow you to heal and be free to move forward into the things of God. God wants you healed so you can walk in clarity. Stand on His Word, which is solid and true.

According to *Merriam-Webster's*, perception is

- the way you think about or understand someone or something
- the ability to understand or notice something easily
- the way that you understand something using one of your senses
- a result of perceiving: observation

- a mental image: concept
- a capacity for comprehension

According to dictionary.com, precaution is

- an action taken to avoid a dangerous or undesirable event
- caution practiced beforehand; circumspection
- a measure taken in advance to avert possible evil or to secure good results
- to forewarn; put on guard

If you were ever raped, that could have destroyed your view of life and made you uncomfortable around all males. You would feel your innocence was gone, and you would lock yourself down emotionally. You would conclude no male could be trusted, and you would act out or withdraw. You would vow that you would never let this happen again! Your vows would get louder and hardened by the pain rehearsing over and over in your mind!

Your perception could set you up for failure in your relationships and marriage. The devil snatched your future and took you on a big detour from God's way. If you don't seek help or help yourself if you can, you end up feeling stuck, and you could have major problems with trust. Your memories, tears, and fears chase you day and night unless you sedate yourself with a quick fix.

There are several defense mechanisms, such as taking precautions throughout life, always being on guard, and never being at rest. You can become a product of the victim's mentality. Come on, that's no way to live. I'm not talking about good precautions because the Lord does not want us not knowing what to do or stay numb to the real issue.

Pray and read God's Word when you face situations; keep your eyes wide open to the truth of God. Jesus loves you so much and hates to see you making decisions based on your fears and shame. The devil is a liar, but Jesus has defeated him. God want us to enjoy life to its fullest and in the abundance of His joy.

Precaution and *perception* are powerful words. They can pattern our lives with fears or personal vows that can bind us up. Your identity is somewhere therein, so fight the good fight of faith with the Word of God. You have the power to break every chain that binds you by speaking His Word and following Jesus's lifestyle. Your perception of life can change with the help of the Lord! Healing is your bread, and there are many benefits in Christ.

Our choices for good or bad will take us on our journeys. Choose to travel with Jesus. God has had a plan for us all right from the beginning. We can find ourselves distracted or delayed, but our purpose remains the same. If we don't stop, we win! Hope mixed with faith pulls us into the light and gets us back in the race. Matthew 24:12–13 (KJV) states, "Because iniquity shall abound, the love of many shall wax cold. But he that shall endure unto the end, the same shall be save. That the race is not to the swift but to the one that endured to the end." When you choose to put down your pain and pick up your purpose, you will be challenged, but you will be victorious.

No matter what the enemy tells you, remember that there's always a way out. Jesus loves you. He died for your sins. He is a forgiving God! John 3:16 (KJV) states, "For God so loved the world, that He gave His only begotten Son, that whosoever believes in Him shall not perish, but have everlasting life." The devil doesn't want you to know this is true. God loves you! When you turn it all over to Jesus, He will work it out. You must obey His Word!

The first thing you should do is forgive. The second thing to do is forgive. The third thing to do is, yes, forgive. To forgive and be forgiven is a gift from God.

Chapter 11

My Prayer of Agreement

Lord, help me! I need Your help today. I can't do this by myself. I thank You for being my Lord and Savior! You loved me before I loved myself. I pray that all my fears and worries are in Your hands. Help me lay aside all my preconceived ideas and precautions that were internalized with pain and caused my life to be on pause at every stop sign. I really should have stopped on life's path and asked questions to get real answers.

My fears, O Lord, kept me from seeking ways of escape, and I ended up back at the same stop sign. There were many times I asked myself, *How long will I continue in the insanity of the same pain?* Lord, with Your wisdom and help, I desire to say yes to yes and no to no. I realize hurts and pain are Your concern as soon as I release them to You. I release it all right now!

As much as I can understand it, I release my memories, scars, pain, hurt, disappointment, and all the lies I can't explain. Now! I can trust You to help me see the best in people. I pray to make a difference with all I've gone through. I refuse to be the victim when You are my God. Renew in me a right spirit that I may not sin against You.

I choose You to help me in all my decisions and choices. You are my shepherd and my protection. Your grace, mercy, and love cover my route and help me focus faithfully on You as my Lord. The desire for revenge is blowing away in this prayer to You. Losing the violence of the touch of change I'm asking for from You helps me daily.

My heart is responding to forgiving myself for everything I engaged in knowingly and unknowingly. In my confession, I deal with me first. Honestly, I repent for anything I've done that's not pleasing to You, my

Lord. I repent for the hurt I've caused to others. I'm sorry. I also repent for thinking that I am in control when I'm not. For seeming to have it all together when I don't.

You are my Savior, and I love You first and foremost. My life without You is nothing. The hour of Your return draws near, and I long to see Your face in peace. I love You so much. You care for me, and You have me on Your mind day and night. My approach to You, Lord, is not always what You want, but as honestly as I can, I surrender myself to You. In this prayer, I vow to serve You for all the days of my life with Your help and guidance. I do love You and desire to please You, Your daughter.

My Signature _____ Your child. You wake me up with a kiss, and because of that, I can see my day and approach it with gratitude. My nights I will no longer fear; I will rest in Your arms of love that drive away all evil. Fear cannot live here anymore. I'm coming out of this because I know You will love the hurt away. You are my healer, and You choose to give me beauty for ashes, oil of joy for mourning, and a garment of praise for the spirit of heaviness.

Help me, O Lord! I put my trust in You. I know no other greater than You. I want to make You my Lord over everything! God, You make everything beautiful in Your time. For that, I love You more than I can say. "To everything there is a season, and a time to every purpose under the heaven" (Ecclesiastes 3:1 KJV).

Encouraging Scripture Reading

Abba, Father (Galatians 4:4–6 KJV): "But when the fulness of the time was, God sent forth his Son, made of a woman, made under the law. To redeem them that were under the law, that we may receive the adoption of sons. Because ye are sons, God hath sent forth the Spirit of his Son into your hearts, crying, Abba, Father."

The Word (John 1:1 KJV): "In the beginning was the Word, and the Word was with God, and the Word was God."

Word of God (Revelation 19:13 KJV): "And he was clothed with a vesture dipped in blood: and his name is called The Word of God."

The Truth (John 1:14 KJV): "And the Word was made flesh, and dwelt among us, (and we beheld his glory, the glory as of the only begotten of the Father), full of grace and truth."

Light of the World (John 8:12 KJV): "Then spake Jesus again unto them, saying, I am the light of the world: he that follow me shall not walk in darkness, but shall have the light of life."

Man of Sorrows (Isaiah 53:3 KJV): "He is despised and rejected of men; a man of sorrows, and acquainted with grief: and we hid as it were our faces from him; he was despised, and we esteemed him not."

Lamb of God (John 1:29 KJV): "The next day John see Jesus coming unto him, and saith, Behold the Lamb of God, which taketh away the sin of the world."

Mediator (1 Timothy 2:5 KJV): "For there is one God, and one mediator between God and men, the man Christ Jesus."

Savior (Luke 2:11 KJV): "For unto you is born this day in the city of David a Savior, which is Christ the Lord."

Author and Finisher of Our Faith (Hebrews 12:2 KJV): "Looking unto Jesus the author and finisher of our faith; who for the joy that was set before him endured the cross, despising the shame, and is set down at the right hand of the throne of God."

First and Last (Revelation 1:17 KJV): "And when I saw him, I fell at his feet as dead. And he laid his right hand upon me, saying unto me, Fear not; I am the first and the last:"

Cornerstone (Psalm 118:22 KJV) "The stone which the builders refused is become the head stone of the corner."

The Door (John 10:7 KJV): "Then said Jesus unto them again, Verily, verily, I say unto you, I am the door of the sheep."

Good Shepherd (John 10:11 KJV): "I am the good shepherd: the good shepherd giveth his life for the sheep."

Great High Priest (Hebrews 4:14 KJV): "Seeing then that we have a great high priest, that is passed into the heavens, Jesus the Son of God, let us hold fast our profession."

Witness (Isaiah 55:4 KJV): "Behold, I have given him for a witness to the people, a leader and commander to the people."

When the time permits, share your story and give God the glory because one woman's cry is another woman's answer.

About the Author

Rosemary is a woman after God's own heart who is gifted and inspired by God to encourage and speak life into the lives of many. She is a God-chosen handmaiden who moves fluently in the prophetic ministry. Being groomed in her early days in Seattle, Washington, Rosemary gifting challenge the God in you to arise, giving you hope with the ability to trust God while executing your purpose and dreams. Rosemary has been married to Arthur Green for more than thirty-nine years. Healed of cancer and was told she would never have children of her own, but God blessed them with three children and one loving stepson whom they love dearly. They moved to Dallas for such a time as this. Through it all, Arthur and Rosemary are grateful to the Lord for His love He has given to their family.

Printed in the United States
By Bookmasters